ROMAN STUDIES HANDBOOK

The Scottish Classics Group

Oliver & Boyd

Oliver & Boyd
Robert Stevenson House
1–3 Baxter's Place
Leith Walk
Edinburgh EH1 3BB

A Division of Longman Group Ltd

First published 1982

ISBN 0 05 003552 5

Set in 11/12 pt Baskerville
Printed in Hong Kong by
Wilture Enterprises (International) Ltd.

Preface

Although the notes that follow have been specially prepared to suit the Latin course *Ecce Romani*, they will undoubtedly be of great value also to those who are preparing courses dealing with the civilisation of ancient Rome, be they in primary or secondary schools. Knowing where to look for material is half the battle.

These are not lists of recommended books nor is it implied that all, or nearly all, are required for any of the topics. They are books which are commonly found in schools and/or books which practising teachers have found helpful. Although some of them are out of print, copies still exist in many schools. The lists are not exhaustive. The books in the lists have a general application; more specialised books on particular subjects are mentioned at the end of each Topic.

How to use this book

The Handbook is divided into two main parts: Section A consists of lists of book titles and audio-visual material together with publishers' names; the books are classified in four separate lists according to difficulty, and each book title is given a code number. Section B contains detailed notes on the usefulness of individual books for the study of particular topics. To find the name of a book, refer to the classified booklists. For example, under the topic Roman Dress, it will be noted that men's dress is dealt with on pages 171–174 of the book whose code number is II. 3, while women's dress is dealt with on pages 187–190 of the same book. By referring to Booklist II, we find that the third book on that list is *Daily Life in Ancient Rome* by Carcopino.

We realise that this can be a very irksome way of referring to books, but to have listed the name of each book every time it is mentioned would have increased the cost of the Handbook considerably.

Contents

Section A
1 Booklists I–IV 5
2 Audio-Visual Aids (General) 11
3 Wallcharts 13
4 Cambridge Latin Course Slides 13
5 Classical Films 14

Section B: Topics
1 Roman Houses 16
2 Roman Dress 20
3 Slavery 21
4 Roads and Travel 23
5 The City of Rome 27
6 Aqueducts 31
7 Roman Food and Eating Habits 33
8 Education 36
9 Roman Drama 39
10 The Baths 41
11 Amphitheatres and the Circus 44
12 Coming of Age 48
13 Weddings 48
14 Funerals 49
15 Clientes 50
16 Pompeii 50
17 Religion 52
18 The Roman Army 54

SECTION A
1 Booklists

Booklist I

This list contains relatively simple books, some of them designed for the primary school. They can be tackled by first-year pupils without much help and direction from the teacher.

I. 1 Heather Amery. *The Time Traveller Book of Rome and Romans*. Usborne.
I. 2 Ella Anderson. *The Story of Ancient Rome*. Odham Books.
I. 3 Martin Ballard. *Rome and Empire A.D. 41–122*. Methuen.
I. 4 C.A. Burland. *Ancient Rome*. Hulton Educational.
I. 5 Trevor Cairns. *The Romans and their Empire*. Cambridge University Press.
I. 6 R. Carrington. *Ancient Rome*. Chatto & Windus.
I. 7 S.L. Case. *Ancient Rome*. Evans.
I. 8 D. Clair. *The Roman Epoch in Britain*. Bruce & Gawthorn.
I. 9 P. E. Cleator. *Finding Out About Rome*. Muller.
I. 10 L.C. Corney. *Story of Ancient Rome*. E.J. Arnold & Son.
I. 11 Jean Defrasne. *History of Ancient Rome*. Burke.
I. 12 G. Derwent. *Roman London*. Macdonald Educational.
I. 13 I. Doncaster. *The Roman Occupation of Britain*. Longman (Evidence in Pictures series).
I. 14 David J. Downton, Melvyn Peavitt & Jon Nichol. *The Romans*. Blackwell.
I. 15 A. Duggan. *The Romans*. Brockhampton Press.
I. 16 Richard Erdoes. *A Picture History of Ancient Rome*. Macmillan.
I. 17 Christopher Fagg. *Ancient Rome*. Longman.
I. 18 Joan Forman. *The Romans*. Macdonald Educational.
I. 19 Lady A. Fox & A. Sorrell. *Roman Britain*. Lutterworth.
I. 20 Emily Frenkel. *Discovering the Classical World*. Pergamon.
I. 21 P. Green. *Look at the Romans*. Hamish Hamilton.
I. 22 Clarence Greig. *Rome*. Ladybird.
I. 23 Stig Hadenius & Birgit Janrup. *How They Lived in Ancient Rome*. Lutterworth.

I. 24 Peter Hodge. *Roman Family Life*. Longman.
I. 25 Peter Hodge. *The Roman House*. Longman.
I. 26 Peter Hodge. *Roman Towns*. Longman.
I. 27 Hugh Hollinghurst. *Greeks and Romans: Topics in Greek and Roman History*. Heinemann.
I. 28 E.C. Kennedy & G.W. White. *S.P.Q.R. (or Publius)*. Macmillan.
I. 29 G. Lawrence. *S.P.Q.R.* Oliver & Boyd.
I. 30 Brenda Lewis. *Growing up in Ancient Rome*. Batsford.
I. 31 Brenda Lewis. *The How and Why Wonder Book of Ancient Rome*. Transworld.
I. 32 D.E. Limebeer. *The Greeks and The Romans: Part 2 The Romans*. Cambridge University Press.
I. 33 J. Lindsay. *Our Roman Heritage*. Weidenfeld & Nicolson.
I. 34 J. Liversidge. *Roman Britain*. Longman (Then and There series).
I. 35 R.D. Lobban. *Roman Britain*. Oliver & Boyd (Quest Library).
I. 36 H.E.L. Mellersh. *Imperial Rome*. Hart-Davis Educational (Young Historian series).
I. 37 E.K. Milliken. *The Roman People*. Harrap.
I. 38 Pierre Miquel. *Life in Ancient Rome*. Hamlyn.
I. 39 R. Mitchell. *At the Time of the Roman Empire*. Longman.
I. 40 R. Mitchell. *Roman Britain*. Longman (Focus on History series).
I. 41 Marie Neurath. *They Lived Like This in the Roman Empire*. Macdonald.
I. 42 R.M. Ogilvie. *Stories from Livy*. Oxford University Press.
I. 43 A. Petrie. *An Introduction to Roman History, Literature and Antiquities*. Oxford University Press.
I. 44 E.R. Pike. *Republican Rome*. Hart-Davis Educational (Young Historian series).
I. 45 Amanda Purves. *Growing Up in Ancient Rome*. Wayland.
I. 46 M. & C.H.B. Quennell. *Everyday Life in Roman and Anglo-Saxon Times*. Batsford.
I. 47 C.E. Robinson. *Ancient Rome*. Ward (First Books series).
I. 48 R.R. Sellman. *Roman Britain*. Methuen (Outlines series).
I. 49 N. Sherwin-White. *Ancient Rome*. Longman (Then and There series).
I. 50 V. Skipp. *Out of the Ancient World*. Penguin.
I. 51 M. Stearns. *The Key to Rome*. Weidenfeld & Nicolson.

I. 52 E.M. Tappan. *The Story of the Roman People*. Harrap.
I. 53 Boswell Taylor (ed). *Ancient Romans*. Knight Books, Hodder & Stoughton.
I. 54 D. Taylor. *Ancient Rome*. Methuen (Outlines series).
I. 55 D. Taylor. *A Soldier on Hadrian's Wall*. Oxford University Press (People of the Past series).
I. 56 O. Thomson. *The Romans in Scotland*. Longman (Then and There series).
I. 57 G. Tingay. *From Caesar to the Saxons*. Longman.
I. 58 G.I.F. Tingay & J. Badcock. *These Were the Romans*. Hulton.
I. 59 Paul Titley. *The Roman World*. Mills & Boon.
I. 60 H.A. Treble & K.M. King. *Everyday Life in Rome*. Oxford University Press.
I. 61 R.J. Unstead. *Greece and Rome*. A. & C. Black.
I. 62 B. Whelpton. *Rome Resplendent*. Burke.
I. 63 V. White. *A Romano-British Family*. Oxford University Press (People of the Past series).
I. 64 Tyler Whittle. *Imperial Rome*. Heinemann.
I. 65 Tyler Whittle. *Royal and Republican Rome*. Heinemann.

Booklist II

This list contains books which are often found in schools but which are rather more difficult and detailed and where help is often required to direct pupils to the information in them. Included here are one or two more expensive books which are well illustrated or, like II. 15, extremely valuable sources of information.

II. 1 Peter Amey. *Pax Romana*. Harrap.
II. 2 A.R. Birley. *Life in Roman Britain*. Batsford (English Life series).
II. 3 J. Carcopino. *Daily Life in Ancient Rome*. Penguin.
II. 4 M. Cary & J. Haarhoff. *Life and Thought in the Greek and Roman World*. Methuen.
II. 5 F.R. Cowell. *Everyday Life in Ancient Rome*. Batsford.
II. 6 O.A.W. Dilke. *The Ancient Romans: How They Lived and Worked*. David & Charles.
II. 7 Eilis Dillon. *Living in Imperial Rome*. Faber.
II. 8 S.J. Freebairn-Smith & G.H. Littlejohn. *From Trial to Triumph, 1: Winner Takes All*. Heinemann.

II. 9 S.J. Freebairn-Smith & G.H. Littlejohn. *From Trial to Triumph, 2: Chief Factors for the Gods*. Heinemann.

II. 10 H. Grose-Hodge. *Roman Panorama*. Cambridge University Press.

II. 11 W.O. Hassall. *How They Lived 55 B.C.–A.D. 1485*. Basil Blackwell.

II. 12 Ruth I. Hicks. *Bonds of Empire: The Roman World in the Age of Trajan*. Macmillan.

II. 13 R.W. Moore. *The Roman Commonwealth*. English Universities Press.

II. 14 R. Nichols & K. McLeish. *Through Roman Eyes*. Cambridge University Press.

II. 15 U.E. Paoli. *Rome: Its People, Life and Customs*. Longman.

II. 16 H.E. Priestley. *Britain Under the Romans*. Warne.

II. 17 Sophie Ramondt. *The Romans*. Lutterworth.

II. 18 John Richardson. *Roman Provincial Administration, 227 B.C. to A.D. 117*. Macmillan.

II. 19 I.A. Richmond. *Roman Britain*. Penguin.

II. 20 *Roman Home Life: An Example of a Topic for Classical Studies*. London Association of Classical Teachers.

II. 21 J.M. Street & A. Chevenix-Trench. *Rome 753 B.C.–A.D. 180*. Blackie.

II. 22 D. Strong. *The Classical World*. Hamlyn.

II. 23 David Taylor. *Cicero and Rome*. Macmillan.

II. 24 J. Wells. *A Short History of Rome to the Death of Augustus*. Methuen.

II. 25 J. Wells & R.H. Barrow. *A Short History of the Roman Empire to the Death of Marcus Aurelius*. Methuen.

II. 26 M. Wheeler. *Roman Art and Architecture*. Thames & Hudson.

II. 27 G.W. White & E.C. Kennedy. *Roman History, Life and Literature*. Macmillan.

II. 28 B. Winer. *Life in the Ancient World*. Thames & Hudson.

II. 29 B.K. Workman. *They Saw it Happen: In Classical Times*. Basil Blackwell.

II. 30 M. Vickers. *The Roman World*. Elsevier-Phaidon.

Booklist III

This list contains books which can be very valuable for both teacher and class but are primarily adult books. Most are available in paperback form.

III. 1 Peter D. Arnott. *An Introduction to the Roman World.* Sphere Books.
III. 2 C. Bailey (ed). *The Legacy of Rome.* Oxford University Press.
III. 3 J.P.V.D. Balsdon. *Life and Leisure in Ancient Rome.* Bodley Head.
III. 4 J.P.V.D. Balsdon (ed). *Roman Civilization.* Penguin.
III. 5 J.P.V.D. Balsdon. *Roman Life and Leisure.* Watts.
III. 6 J.P.V.D. Balsdon. *Roman Women: Their History and Habits.* Bodley Head.
III. 7 J.P.V.D. Balsdon (ed). *The Romans.* Watts.
III. 8 R.H. Barrow. *The Romans.* Penguin.
III. 9 M. Cary & H.H. Scullard. *A History of Rome Down to the Reign of Constantine.* Macmillan.
III. 10 M.P. Charlesworth. *The Roman Empire.* Oxford University Press (Opus).
III. 11 Marcus Tullius Cicero. *Respublica: Roman Politics and Society According to Cicero.* Selected and translated by W.K. Lacey and B.W.J.G. Wilson. Bristol Classical Press.
III. 12 Marcus Tullius Cicero. *Selected Political Speeches of Cicero.* Translated by Michael Grant. Penguin.
III. 13 F.R. Cowell. *Cicero and the Roman Republic.* Penguin.
III. 14 Sir S. Dill. *Roman Society from Nero to Marcus Aurelius.* Meridian.
III. 15 Donald R. Dudley. *The Civilization of Rome.* Mentor Books.
III. 16 Donald R. Dudley. *Roman Society.* Penguin.
III. 17 M.I. Finley. *Aspects of Antiquity: Discoveries and Controversies.* Penguin.
III. 18 Michael Grant. *The Climax of Rome.* Cardinal-Sphere Books.
III. 19 Michael Grant. *The Fall of the Roman Empire: A Reappraisal.* Nelson.
III. 20 Michael Grant (ed). *Latin Literature.* Penguin.
III. 21 Michael Grant. *The World of Rome.* Sphere Books.
III. 22 G. Highet. *Poets in a Landscape.* Pelican Books.

III. 23 *Inscriptions of the Roman Empire A.D. 14–117.* London Association of Classical Teachers.
III. 24 N. Lewis & M. Reinhold. *Roman Civilization: A Source Book.* Vol. I – *The Republic*, Vol. II – *The Empire.* Harper & Row (Torch Books).
III. 25 M.P. Nilsson. *Imperial Rome.* Schocken: Bailey Bros.
III. 26 R.M. Ogilvie. *Early Rome and the Etruscans.* Harvester Press.
III. 27 J.C. & H.G. Robertson. *The Story of Greece and Rome: Their Growth and Their Legacy to Our Western World.* Dent.
III. 28 *Roman Politics: Sources from the History of the Late Republic.* London Association of Classical Teachers.
III. 29 M. Rostovtzeff. *Rome.* Galaxy Books.
III. 30 H.H. Scullard. *From the Gracchi to Nero.* Methuen.
III. 31 A. Stenico. *Roman and Etruscan Painting.* Weidenfeld & Nicolson.
III. 32 David Stockton. *Cicero: A Political Biography.* Oxford University Press.
III. 33 David Taylor. *Work in Ancient Greece and Rome.* Allen & Unwin.
III. 34 W. Warde Fowler. *Rome.* Oxford University Press (Opus).
III. 35 W. Warde Fowler. *Social Life at Rome in the Age of Cicero.* Macmillan.
III. 36 Alan Wardman. *Rome's Debt to Greece.* Elek.

Booklist IV

This list contains books which are very expensive, and individual departments in the normal course of events could not be expected to have them.

IV. 1 M. Brion. *Pompeii and Herculaneum.* Elek Books.
IV. 2 G. Gianelli (ed). *The World of Ancient Rome.* Macdonald & Co Ltd.
IV. 3 M. Grant (ed). *The Birth of Western Civilisation.* Thames & Hudson.
IV. 4 P. Grimal. *The Civilisation of Rome.* Allen & Unwin.
IV. 5 P. Grimal and others. *Hellenism and the Rise of Rome.* Weidenfeld & Nicolson.

IV. 6 M. Hadas. *Imperial Rome*. Time-Life International.
IV. 7 Joan Liversidge. *Britain in the Roman Empire*. Routledge & Kegan Paul.
IV. 8 A.H. McDonald. *Republican Rome*. Thames & Hudson.
IV. 9 Lino Rossi. *Trajan's Column and the Dacian Wars*. Thames & Hudson.
IV. 10 Sir J.E. Sandys. *A Companion to Latin Studies*. Hafner Publishing.
IV. 11 J.M.C. Toynbee. *Animals in Roman Life and Art*. Thames & Hudson.
IV. 12 A.A.M. van der Heyden & H.H. Scullard. *Atlas of the Classical World*. Nelson.

It is worth adding that for most of the background topics a concise explanation will be found under the relevant heading in the *Oxford Classical Dictionary*, and relevant quotations will be found in the index to Lewis & Reinhold's *Roman Civilization*, Volumes I and II (Harper & Row, Torch books).

2 Audio-Visual Aids (General)

All the following are supplied with teacher's notes and all are in colour.

The Ancient World No. 4: Rome and the Empire. Longman, Common Ground (Filmstrip).
City and Empire; aqueducts and public buildings; arts; views around the Empire. These are of high quality.

Aspects of Roman Life. AV Productions (Slides).
Collection of busts, wall paintings and mosaics, mainly from Pompeii and Piazza Armerina, illustrating aspects of life, house decoration; 4 slides relate to the Villa of Mysteries at Pompeii.

Early Civilisations: Greece and Rome. Slide Centre.
Only eight colour slides of the set are relevant.

Great Civilisations: Rome. Ladybird (Filmstrip).
24 artist's drawings depict the history and life of the Romans as in the Ladybird book.
Imperial Rome. EAV (Filmstrip).
40 frames permit a wide coverage of many aspects of Rome and the Romans.
Imperium Romanum. Encyclopaedia Britannica (Filmstrip).
Informative treatment with captions on frames – maps, photographs and reconstructed scenes are included.
Life in Roman Britain. Slide Centre (Slides).
Artist's drawings offer some useful illustrations for villa, amphitheatre, road building, meals, baths and trades.
Life in the Roman Empire. Longman, Common Ground (Filmstrip).
Illustrates defence, travel, entertainment, buildings and religion in the course of 32 frames.
People in Roman Times. EAV (Filmstrip).
Includes views of buildings, dress, schooling, entertainments, food and religion.
A Roman City: 1 Streets and Monuments. AV Productions (Slides).
12 views show streets and buildings in Rome, Pompeii and Herculaneum.
A Roman City: 2 Daily Life. AV Productions (Slides).
24 slides show bridges, aqueducts, arches, tombs, public buildings, entertainment and trades.
Roman Civilization. EAV (Tape, 2 filmstrips).
Illustrates in two filmstrips with tape the art and architecture of Rome and the organisation of the Empire. Various aspects are examined.
The Roman Empire. Coronet Filmstrips (Filmstrips).
Four filmstrips with cassettes examine the history of Rome and its various achievements.
The Roman Republic. EAV (Tape, filmstrip).
Follows Rome's history from the time of the kings to the rise of Augustus – numerous topics included.
Roman Society. EAV (Filmstrips).
Two filmstrips consider various categories of Roman society and their various occupations.
Rome: The Eternal City. Part 1: Kings and Consuls. Life Filmstrips.
Rome's growth is illustrated with captions on frames from Etruscans to Julius Caesar: buildings, roads, aqueducts and theatres are included.

Rome: The Eternal City. Part 2: The Emperors. Life Filmstrips.
Single frame with captions and notes on frames. Buildings, literature and other works associated with Emperors, especially Augustus, Hadrian, Antoninus Pius and Marcus Aurelius.

Verulamium. Kay (Filmstrip).
40 frames; colour. Interesting selection covers various topics, and not confined to Roman Britain.

3 Wallcharts

Various maps illustrating Italy and Rome are available from Westermann, Breasted-Huth-Harding (distributor George Philip & Son) and Haack Gotha (distributor Pergamon/Wheaton).

Pictorial Education Monthly and Quarterly produce pictures and charts of relevance fairly regularly.

4 Cambridge Latin Course Slides

The Cambridge Latin Course publishes an extensive and high-quality collection of slides with each of the five units of the course. These can be purchased independently of the course. They cover a wide range of topics and can be strongly recommended. Items of relevance to the background topics in the following pages include:

Houses and Decoration	Set **I** – numerous frames:
(a) *Villa Urbana*	**II** 3–14: **II** 33–35: **II** 36–38: **IV** 17: **IV** 18 Pliny's Laurentine Villa: **V** 39–40.

(b) *Villa Rustica* — **I** 36: **III** 34: **III** 35: **IV** 2.72, 74, 75, 76, 77: **V** 8, 9, 11, 12.

(c) *Insula* — **III** 27, 28.

Pompeii — Set **I** – many frames: **V** 35, 36, 37.

Dress — **I** 1: **II** 24: **II** 25: **III** 67, 68: **IV** 2.52, 55, 59, 60, tombs, portraits, busts.

Slavery — **I** 36, 37, 45: **II** 40, 41: **III** 3, 8: **V** 42.

Money — **II** 53, 69, 71–74: **V** 25, 26, 27.

Transport — **I** 19, 32, 44: **III** 37, 41, 42, 43, 44: **IV** 27.

Roads — **I** 27, 28, 29, 30, 31: **III** 26.

Rome — **III** 19, 20, 21, 23, 24, 25, 26, 31: **IV** 28, 29, 30, 31, 32, 40.

Water & Aqueducts — **III** 30, 31, 37.

Food & Eating — **I** 9, 16, 17, 19, 23, 24, 35, 39: **II** 49, 50: **IV** 23: **IV** 2.74, 75, 76, 77: **V** 5.

Education — **II** 31: **IV** 25: **IV** 2.57, 58.

Theatre — **I** 46, 47, 48, 49.

Baths — **I** 55, 56, 57, 58, 59: **II** 5: **III** 1, 2, 3.

Amphitheatre — **I** 50, 51, 52, 53: **II** 51: **III** 23, 24: **IV** 13

Wedding — **III** 55.

Death & Funerals — **II** 59, 60: **III** 7, 15, 16, 17: **III** 56, 57, 58, 59, 60, 61, 62: **IV** 2.51, 60, 62.

Religion — **I** 5, 20: **II** 27–30: **III** 4–6, 50–54: **IV** 8, 9: **IV** 2.62.

Army — **II** 1, 53–60: **III** 9–14, 18, 22, 69, 73, 74: **IV** 38.

5 Classical Films

There are several 16 mm films relating to the classical world which are available for hire or purchase. Excluding epics of the cinema such as *Quo Vadis?* or *Ben Hur*, the following lists some of the better examples.

(a) Most of these are of a general nature and range across many topics:

Roman Britain: Towns. Baddeley. 15 minutes; colour.
A useful and wide-ranging introductory film. A filmstrip showing stills of the film is available.

Roman Provincial Society: Domestic. Gateway. 25 minutes; colour.
A well-produced film with wide coverage; recommended.

The Spirit of Rome. Encyclopaedia Britannica. 29 minutes; colour.
A well-produced film but fairly demanding in its coverage. It is a fairly mature treatment.

The Roman World. Boulton Hawker. 22 minutes; colour.
The film ranges across the monuments in various parts of the Roman Empire.

The Romans. Patterson Associates. 26 minutes; colour.
This is another wide-ranging film covering the whole empire.

Life in Ancient Rome. Encyclopaedia Britannica. 14 minutes; colour.
The film covers many aspects of life, work and leisure in ancient Rome.

Claudius, Boy of Ancient Rome. Encyclopaedia Britannica. 16 minutes; colour.
An attractive little film on the life of a Roman youngster. A filmstrip showing stills of this film is a useful adjunct for purposes of recall.

(b) The following films relate more particularly to topics covered in the following sections:

The Buried Cities. Boulton Hawker. 14 minutes; colour.
Good material on Pompeii and Herculaneum, but now rather dated.

Spartacus. Extracts from feature film. British Film Institute. 30 minutes; colour.
Extracts cover life and fighting, slaves in mine and country, the battle sequence. Suitable for all ages.

Roman Britain: Fortification. Baddeley. 14 minutes; colour.
Suitable for all ages, it covers many aspects of the military occupation. A filmstrip showing stills of the film is also available.

SECTION B
Topics

1 Roman Houses

The same basic points are made about Roman houses in almost all the books listed. However, as the amount of additional detail varies very widely from book to book, in addition to exact references, we try to indicate the scope of the coverage. Books on Roman Britain are often as useful as books on Rome in general, as they tend to contain information which is generally applicable to the whole Roman world.

Booklist

I. 1, pp. 6–7	Roman streets and buildings – artist's reconstruction and brief text interspersed.
I. 1, pp. 8–9	Roman house, Pompeian style – artist's drawing of rooms with text interspersed.
I. 8, pp. 34–39	Deals with houses in towns with fairly good detail.
I. 8, pp. 41–44	Gives a very simple account of 'villas' in Roman Britain.
I. 10, pp. 40–42	A general and fairly brief account.
I. 12, pp. 98–100	A good section on furniture.
I. 17, pp. 12–13	Country villa and simple account of farming.
I. 18, pp. 14–19	Cut-away of town house, photos and pictures with brief text.
I. 19, pp. 30–33	Not much text but the pictures contain a great deal of information.
I. 25	All chapters are relevant.
I. 26, pp. 21–29	Streets, houses and shops.
I. 28, pp. 12–15	A few details of a Pompeian-type house worked into the story.

I. 32, pp. 47, 83	Very limited information.
I. 33, pp. 82–95	Deals with the countryside of Roman Britain and villas in particular.
I. 34, pp. 55–64	Much of general interest and application although concern is particularly with Roman Britain.
I. 35, pp. 9–10	Deals with houses in Romano-British towns.
I. 35, pp. 13–18	Deals with houses in the country.
I. 37, pp. 38–39	A simple account, very limited in context.
I. 39, pp. 40–57	Roman houses and their furnishings simply but well presented.
I. 43, pp. 113–115	A very short concentrated account.
I. 46, pp. 55–63	A very close-written and fairly detailed account; not easy to read.
I. 47, pp. 20–22	A very brief description.
I. 48, pp. 38–40	A short account of villas in Roman Britain.
I. 49, pp. 36–38, 77–78	A very basic introduction.
I. 53, pp. 11–15	Town house, tenement and villa (mainly illustration).
I. 57, Chs. 15–16	Deals with town and country in Roman Britain but contains a lot of information.
I. 60, pp. 30–43	The first part of the chapter is a general description; pp. 35–40 deal with a visit to the house of the Vettii which would be excellent if accompanied by slides of the various features mentioned; pp. 40–43 deal with houses in the country.
I. 63	This is elementary in style but contains good information scattered throughout the whole booklet.
II. 2, Ch. 5	Is concerned with the Romano-British countryside but many references to farms and houses are scattered throughout.

II. 3, pp. 33–57	A great amount of information on many aspects of Roman houses. Pupils require a certain amount of direction if they are not to become overwhelmed by the wealth of detail in these pages.
II. 5, p. 18 seq.	Mainly concerned with Rome itself.
II. 10, pp. 179–193	A very useful chapter.
II. 13, pp. 83–90	A clear and reasonably detailed account.
II. 15, Chs. 2–3	Excellent information; the second on the villa.
II. 26	Both text and illustration are useful, particularly the pictures on pp. 184–185.
II. 27, pp. 184–191	A straightforward account, less detailed than the other books in this list.
III. 3, pp. 193–211	Country villas.
III. 7, pp. 163–169	A straightforward account.
III. 13, p. 87	A few interesting facts on building.
III. 14, pp. 175–181	Concerned with the villas mentioned by Pliny and Statius.
III. 22, pp. 133–147	A rather discursive attempt to evoke the spirit of Horace's villa.
III. 31	Some of the wall paintings from houses.
III. 35, Ch. 8	Good information about Cicero and his country residences.
IV. 1	Has many valuable illustrations and a wealth of material.
IV. 2	Has good pictures and a simple text.
IV. 4	Chapter 7 (especially pp. 321–351) and Chapter 8 for towns.
IV. 7	Chapters 9 and 10 are packed with information.
IV. 8	Page 129 onwards has information on archaeological sites which is not readily available elsewhere.
IV. 12	Page 122 has an excellent diagram of a house.

Additional books

Calza-Becatti. *Ostia* (in the Guide-books to the Museums and Monuments of Italy).

B.W. Cunliffe. *Fishbourne*. Thames & Hudson.

L.A. & J.A. Hamey. *The Roman Engineers*. Penguin Books. Ch. 5 has a useful and informative section on building materials.

A.G. McKay. *Houses, Villas and Palaces in the Roman World*. Thames & Hudson.

A. Maiuri. *Pompeii* and *Herculaneum* (in the Guide-books to the Museums and Monuments of Italy).

Lt.-Col. G.W. Meates. *Lullingstone Roman Villa*. Heinemann. An account of an excavation in Kent. (A film of this is available for hire and a Ministry of Works guide may be obtained from H.M.S.O.).

R. Meiggs. *Roman Ostia*. Oxford University Press. A very useful book.

A.L.F. Rivet. *Town and Country in Roman Britain*. Hutchinson's University Library. Has material for Roman Britain.

A.L.F. Rivet (ed.). *The Roman Villa in Britain*. Routledge & Kegan Paul. Definitive study of this specialist area.

D.S. Robertson. *Greek and Roman Architecture*. Cambridge University Press. Pp. 297–321, Ch. 17 relate specifically to housing.

For teachers who read Italian, the publications of the Instituto geografico de Agostini-Novara have excellent pictures, e.g. *Pompei: La Città Dissepolata*.

Audio-visual material

Appreciation of Architecture, part 3: Roman Architecture. Visual Publications (Filmstrip).

B/w double frames include reconstructions of town houses and tenements.

Life in Roman Britain: Roman Country Life. AV Productions (Overhead transparencies).

Bignor Roman villa, hypocaust, granary and farming are illustrated.

People of Other Days: 2 The Roman Villa. Visual Publications (Filmstrip).
Depicts life in Romano-British villa by means of artist's drawings. Touches on country crafts and farming.
Roman Architecture. AV Productions (Slides).
20 slides illustrate major monuments in Rome.
A Roman House. AV Productions (Slides).
24 slides show buildings and art in Pompeii and Herculaneum.
Roman House. Daily Mail EFVA (Filmstrip). 37 frames, b/w.
Roman Villa. Visual Publications Ltd. (Filmstrip). 26 frames, colour.
The Roman House. EAV (Filmstrip).
Concerned mainly with the town house, its rooms and furnishing. Provides a useful study.
Villas in Roman Britain. Jackdaw Publication.
Provides pictures, charts and study material on this specialist area.

2 Roman Dress

Booklist

I. 12, pp. 100–105	An excellent short account with line drawings.
I. 18, pp. 22–23	Clothes and fashion illustrated and briefly described.
I. 24, pp. 36–46	Useful chapter on dress and fashion.
I. 38, pp. 54–55	Two pages with very useful illustrations.
I. 39, pp. 20–24	Brief account with illustrations.
I. 40, p. 25	Good clear photograph of a **toga**.
I. 43, pp. 115–118	Useful detail in a short section.
I. 53, pp. 2–3	Clothes and fashion, army dress – mainly illustrations.
I. 60, Ch. 5	
I. 61, pp. 49–50	Brief account with illustrations – relates to men and women.
II. 3, pp. 171–174	Men.
II. 3, pp. 187–190	Women.

Additional books

H. Russell Robinson. *What the Soldiers Wore on Hadrian's Wall.* Graham.
Well illustrated, inexpensive booklet, written by an authority on the subject.
Marian Sichel. *Costume of the Classical World.* Batsford.

Audio-visual material

People in Roman Times. EAV (Filmstrip).
Contains a few relevant frames on this topic.

3 Slavery

It is difficult to find information on slaves collected together in any one book – especially in the most elementary books suitable for pupils at this stage. Books on Roman Britain tend to be less helpful on this topic than on housing. Almost all the books in the booklists have references to slavery but they are often so scattered throughout the books that there is little profit in giving them here. Only references to collected information are given. As with so many of these topics, the *Oxford Classical Dictionary* provides basic information.

Booklist

I. 17, pp. 24–26	Account of slaves and citizens – a rather summary mention.
I. 28, pp. 38–44	Makes a number of good points in the fictional style of this book.
I. 32, pp. 68–69	A very limited amount of information.
I. 60, Ch. 10	A good and fairly full chapter.
II. 3, Ch. 3	From section 2 onwards is concerned in the main with slaves. There is an enormous amount of detail but it requires some selection as the chapter as a whole is concerned with the whole Roman social structure.

II. 4, pp. 127–131	
II. 5, Ch. 4	Is a comprehensive account.
II. 13, pp. 73–76	A factual account with the basic information.
II. 15, Ch. 10	Is a detailed account of slaves.
II. 17, pp. 63–71	Fairly full account in simple terms.
II. 27, pp. 216–218	
III. 3, pp. 106–115	
III. 6, pp. 230–234	In the main a discussion of marriage in relation to slaves; probably best for teacher's reference only at this stage.
III. 7, Ch. 9	Gives a good account.
III. 10, pp. 50–52	Gives a summary of the position of slaves.
III. 14, Ch. 3	A whole chapter is devoted to freedom in this book but it would require a good deal of selection and direction if used for pupil consultation.
III. 17, pp. 154–166	Informative account.
III. 21, pp. 109–125	A very good account containing much from the sources.
III. 24	These volumes contain a large number of passages from which the teacher would require to make his own selection of those most suitable for his purpose.
III. 30, pp. 13–14, 185, 334	
p. 95	Is concerned with the Spartacus revolt.
III. 35, passim, esp. Ch. 7	Much good material but very wordy.
IV. 4	Slaves are not treated as a separate topic but have an important place in the chapter on 'Rome and the Land' (p. 230 in particular) and 'Rome, Queen of Cities' (p. 303 in particular).
IV.7, pp. 15–19	Has a short readable account referring to the evidence from Britain.

Additional books

W.W. Buckland. *Roman Laws of Slavery*. Cambridge University Press.

M.I. Finley. *Slavery in Classical Antiquity*. Heffer.

Kenneth Hughes. *Slavery*. Allen & Unwin.
Suitable for middle school.

Michael Massey & Paul Moreland. *Slavery in Ancient Rome*. Macmillan.
A very good account suitable for middle school.

Audio-visual material

Roman Society, Part 2. EAV (Filmstrip).
Section deals with slaves and freedom.

Slaves in Ancient Rome. EAV (Tape, Filmstrip).
Directly relevant to the topic and a valuable resource.

Two Boys of Ancient Rome. Encyclopaedia Britannica (Filmstrip).
Follows events in the film *Claudius, Boy of Ancient Rome* and makes for useful recall of wide range of aspects of life in Rome. Captions appear on frames.

4 Roads and Travel

Booklist

I. 13, p. 26	Two photographs of Roman roads.
I. 14, pp. 30–33	Pictures and accounts of roads in Britain and their construction.
I. 18, pp. 40–41	Road construction and forms of transport: illustration and brief text.
I. 19, pp. 13–15	A brief reference in the text and a useful drawing of Romans building a road through woodland.
I. 28, pp. 54–57	An imaginative reconstruction of a journey in a **raeda**.
I. 29, pp. 81–85	A brief account of road building and the importance of roads,

	incorporating an account of Horace's journey to Brundisium. Also mentions some of the travellers to be found on roads.
I. 30, Ch. 8	Useful section on this topic.
I. 34, pp. 77–78	Details of a Roman road.
I. 35, pp. 31–36	An elementary account of roads but has some information on travellers and trade.
I. 38, pp. 48–51	Four pages relate to this topic with useful illustrations.
I. 46, pp. 105–111	Some good information but mixed with some dubious statements and irrelevant detail. There is a useful drawing of a milestone and its inscription.
I. 48, pp. 38–40	Road making.
I. 48, p. 42	A short paragraph on trade.
I. 48, p. 64	The canal system in Britain.
I. 49, pp. 80–83	Roads and the army, with some details of travel culled from Pliny.
I. 49, pp. 60–61	Sea transport.
I. 53, p. 27	Roman civil engineering – mainly illustrations.
I. 56, pp. 70–77	Deals with a merchant and the type of goods which he might be carrying for soldiers on frontier duty and their dependants.
I. 57, pp. 92–98	An excellent chapter on roads, particularly in Britain.
I. 60, pp. 90–97	A straightforward account of roads, inns and travel by land and sea.
II. 2, pp. 98, 131	Illustration of vehicles.
II. 4, pp. 132–137	Travel by sea, river, canal and road.
II. 5, pp. 114–116	Contains a good deal of information on transport and travel in very small compass.
II. 6, Ch. 4	An interesting account of the Roman transport network.
II. 10, pp. 129–130	A very simple account of road building.
II. 13, pp. 206–210	Travel in general followed by a survey

		of the Empire in the form of a journey.
II. 15,	pp. 228–231	Gives good detail of the vehicles used.
II. 16,	pp. 25–31	Deals with the construction of roads using the **groma**. Mentions and explains the 'Antonine Itinerary'.
II. 25,	pp. 312–324	Roads, with special reference to trade.
II. 27,	pp. 178–181	A useful short account of roads, inns, and postal service.
III. 2,	pp. 141–161	A general account of communication and commerce; pages 159–161 deal with **tabellarii, diploma**, etc.
III. 3,	Ch. 7, pp. 224–243	
III. 7,	pp. 146–147	A good description of road making.
III. 8,	pp. 98–100	One or two facts about trade and movement of people.
III. 10,	pp. 81–91	A chapter on the wealth of the Empire, trade and travel.
III. 14,	pp. 205–207	Some interesting remarks on length of journeys, desire to travel and comfort in travelling.
III. 16,	pp. 225–227	Brief but colourful references.
III. 24,	Vol. II, pp. 153–155	Some inscriptions commemorating the building of roads.
III. 27,	pp. 207–222	Pp. 211 onwards contain a simple, clear account of the Roman road network including many of the names of the roads.
III. 30,	pp. 342–344	A brief summary.
IV. 2,	pp. 245–264	A very detailed and well illustrated account of travel, first by land, then by sea.
IV. 4,	p. 493	An account of roads – illustrations 207–212 are of roads; 77, 94, 129 and 130 are of vehicles. Page 259 has a map naming all the roads leading from Rome.
IV. 6,	pp. 163–164	A brief account. There is also a picture of the Via Appia on p. 17.
IV. 7,	pp. 381–419	Contains detailed information on many aspects of Roman roads

and their uses. The examples are taken from Britain but the information applies to the whole Empire.

IV. 12, pp. 120–121 Pictures of roads and means of travel. Page 129 has ships and p. 128 has maps with the roads marked.

Additional books

David Birt. *Roads, Travel and Trade*. Longman.
Part of a larger unit, *The Romans in Britain*.

Lionel Casson. *Travel in the Ancient World*. Allen & Unwin.
Informative and wide-ranging account. Pp. 115–239: Travel and touring in Roman times; pp. 163–175: Roman roads; pp. 176–196: Travel by road.

Raymond Chevallier. *Roman Roads*. Batsford.
Detailed and informative study.

Georges Cyrille. *Roman Roads*. Hart-Davis Educational.
A book suitable for younger readers.

T. Falcon-Barker. *A Roman Galley Beneath the Sea*. Brockhampton Press.

L.A. & J.A. Hamey. *The Roman Engineers*. Penguin Books.
Ch. 3 contains an excellent section on roads; p. 28 deals briefly with the port of Ostia; Ch. 4 deals with bridges.

Peter Hodge. *Roman Trade and Travel*. Longman.
Suitable for use by pupils.

Firmin O'Sullivan. *The Egnatian Way*. David & Charles.
Written with the tourist in mind as well as the specialist.

J.H. Peel. *Along the Roman Roads of Britain*. Pan Books.

T.H. Rowland. *Dere Street: Roman Road North from York to Scotland*. Graham.
Informative booklet on one famous road.

T.H. Rowland. *Roman Transport in the North of England*. Graham

V.W. Von Hagen. *Roman Roads*. Rupert Hart-Davis.
Contains much information, not only about roads but about places on them.

Philip Warner. *Roman Roads*. Wayland.
Comprehensive account which extends into life in the Empire. Suitable for use by pupils.

Two simple books which refer to travel in Roman times are *Travel by Road* and *Travel by Sea* in Blackie's Junior Reference Library. The introduction to I.D. Margary, *Roman Roads in Britain* (Baker Ltd) and Chapter 1 of R.C. Collingwood and I. Richmond, *The Archaeology of Roman Britain* (Methuen) are both excellent and contain reliable information.

Audio-visual material

Life in the Roman Empire. Longman, Common Ground (Filmstrip).
Frames 19–21 on travel.

People of Other Days: 3, Roman Roads. Visual Publications (Filmstrip).
Consists of artist's drawings relating to Roman Britain in particular. Illustrates the building and use of the road system.

Ecce Romani Posters: Set 1 *Travel by Land*, Set 2 *Travel by Sea*. Oliver & Boyd.

5 The City of Rome

To find good accounts of the actual city of Rome it is necessary to go to more specialised books than those in this booklist. Hence only a few titles are mentioned.

Booklist

I. 17, pp. 16–17	A very brief description of Rome.
I. 18, pp. 36–37	Brief and general description.
I. 28, pp. 33–37	A walk through the city.
I. 38, pp. 28–29	Living in Rome – two pages with illustrations.
I. 39, pp. 4–15	An interesting and lively account with illustrations.
I. 51	The first chapters are concerned with ancient Rome; the book has one or two useful photographs.
I. 53, pp. 18–19	Map of Rome and illustrations.

I. 60, Ch. 2	An imaginary tour of the city as it was in the time of Caesar. A tour like this is difficult to visualise unless one has visited the place and such an account really requires to be read in conjunction with the showing of slides of the places mentioned.
I. 62, Ch. 3 & 5	Could be useful.
II. 3, Ch. 1 & 2	Both chapters deal with the layout and appearance of ancient Rome in great detail. These are really chapters for the teacher and, if reference is to be made by pupils, this should be to find out specific points.
II. 5, pp. 13–18	These pages of the first chapter are concerned with the building of Rome.
II. 10, Ch. 3	A sketch of the historical development of the city. One or two famous buildings are mentioned and there is an impression of the poorer quarters based on Juvenal.
II. 15, Ch. 1	An excellent chapter on the city.
II. 15, Ch. 13	An account of streets and addresses.
II. 22, pp. 144–146	Some useful coloured pictures.
II. 22, pp. 150–151	
II. 25, pp. 18–19	Building under Augustus.
II. 25, pp. 218–219	Building under Trajan.
II. 25, pp. 248–249	Building under Hadrian.
II. 26	There are several useful plates of buildings and landmarks.
II. 27, Part III, Chs. 1, 2, 4, 5	Chapter 1 is on Rome and its topography and is in the form of a conducted tour starting from the Janiculan Hill, then crossing the Tiber and proceeding to the **Forum Romanum**. In Chapter 2 we have some of the large public buildings. Chapter 4 deals with triumphal arches and Chapter 5 with aqueducts.

III. 2, pp. 383–474	In these chapters on architecture, building and engineering are many references (with diagrams and photographs) to famous buildings in Rome.
III. 13, p. 33	An interesting short paragraph on conditions in Rome.
III. 21, Ch. 10	Mainly concerned with architecture.
III. 22, Ch. 8	Some information on Rome.
III. 24, Vol. I, p. 409	Legislation by Caesar on roads in the city.
Vol. II, pp. 67–69	Quotation from Suetonius' 'Augustus'
III. 25, p. 252	A brief account of public buildings.
III. 35, Ch. 1 & pp. 28–32	Chapter 1 is a comment on the site of Rome followed by a tour through the Forum. The second reference is to **insulae**.
IV. 2, Ch. 1	Is concerned with Rome in the Augustan Age.
IV. 4, Ch. 8	A very clear account of many of the features of ancient Rome with diagrams and maps showing the extension of the city at historical periods, descriptions of the Capitol, the **Forum Romanum** and later **Fora**, the Palatine, theatres, baths and aqueducts.
IV. 6, pp. 7–23	Is the main treatment of Rome in the book.
IV. 6, pp. 147–151	Life of the city, shops, etc.
IV. 8, Ch. 7	Is on 'Monuments of Republican Rome' and is a fairly bare summary which requires a plan to follow easily.
IV. 12, pp. 138–147	Contains pictures including air photographs and a plan of Rome.

Additional books

Anthony Birley. *Imperial Rome*. Lutterworth.
Illustrated by Sorrell, it is a marvellous guide to the buildings of ancient Rome.

F.E. Brown. *Roman Architecture*. Studio Vista.
Has some good pictures and refers to many of the buildings in Rome. It has a detailed bibliography.
Russell Chamberlin. *Rome*. Time-Life International.
Eleanor Clark. *Rome and a Villa*. Ellis.
Splendid guide to Rome and Hadrian's villa.
D.R. Dudley. *Urbs Roma*. Phaidon Press.
A collection and selection of documentary evidence, both from inscriptions and literature of the City of Rome in ancient times. It is an extremely valuable work in that it contains much that cannot be easily found elsewhere. There are also some excellent black and white illustrations.
Helen & Richard Leacroft. *The Buildings of Ancient Rome*. Brockhampton.
A useful book for use by pupils.
P. Leprohon. *Rome*. W.H. Allen (World of Wonderful Places series).
David Macaulay. *City: A Story of Roman Planning and Construction*. Collins.
Excellent book to illustrate buildings and life in ancient Rome.
Richard & Barbara Mertz. *Two Thousand Years in Rome*. Dent.
Detailed guide to Rome over the ages.
T.W. Mulryne. *The Roman Forum*. Bell & Hyman.
A useful handbook for the intending visitor.
Nora Nowlan. *The Tiber: The Roman River*. Muller.
Attractive account from a different viewpoint.
A. Pereira. *Rome*. Batsford.
Stewart Perowne. *Rome: From its Foundation to the Present Day*. Elek.
Lino Rossi. *Trajan's Column and the Dacian Wars*. Thames & Hudson.
Detailed description of one famous monument in Rome.
William M. Seaman & Carolyn J. Matzke. *Forum Romanum*. American Classical League.
Informative guide to the buildings in the Forum.
J.J.M. Timmers. *The Glory of Rome: An Explorer's Guide*. Elsevier-Phaidon.
Fine illustrations capture the feeling of Rome today.
Malcolm Todd. *Walls of Rome*. Elek.

Audio-visual material

Ancient Rome. Gateway (Filmstrip).
A most attractive study of classical remains in modern Rome.

Architectura Romana. Encyclopaedia Britannica (Filmstrip).
A very useful strip with captions (Latin or English) on frames. Illustrates features of construction and shows original buildings and reconstructions.

The Glory that was Rome. Focal Point (Filmstrip).
Buildings and art treasures in Rome, Pompeii and other parts of the Empire.

The Growth of Rome. Longman,· Common Ground (Filmstrip).
A useful summary from earliest times and touches on several topics of interest.

Historical Reconstructions of Rome. Encyclopaedia Britannica (Study prints with overlays).
A most attractive, if expensive, set of prints with reconstruction overlays.

Imperial Rome. EAV (Filmstrip).
40 frames cover a wide range of aspects of Rome.

Roma Antiqua. Centaur Books (Postcard set).
12 black and white views.

Roman Architecture. AV Productions (Slide set).

Rome. AV Productions (OHT: base and 3 overlays – maps).
Base shows Rome and 7 hills; overlay 1 includes major Republican additions, overlay 2 relates to Empire and overlay 3 to Christian Rome.

6 Aqueducts

Booklist

I. 1, pp. 18–19	Illustrations of construction and brief text.
I. 17, pp. 28–31	Good account with illustrations.
I. 18, pp. 34–35	The building of aqueducts: text and illustration.
I. 26, pp. 41–51	Especially pp. 41–43 for aqueducts.
I. 37, pp. 31–32	Brief account.
I. 39, p. 36	Illustration of Pont du Gard.

II. 5,	pp. 100–101	A brief account of Rome's water supplies.
II. 29,	pp. 178–181	Quotations from Frontinus.
IV. 2,	p. 92	Illustration of aqueduct at Segovia.
IV. 2,	p. 251	Pont du Gard.
IV. 4,	pp. 293–297	An account of the Roman system: see also the paragraph on aqueducts (p. 422). Illustrations Nos. 115–117.
IV. 6,	pp. 162–163	Some useful explanatory drawings: p. 31 has a black and white picture of the Segovia aqueduct.

Additional books

D.R. Dudley. *Urbs Roma*. Phaidon.
Pages 38–42 give some of the inscriptions and a short account of the aqueducts.

Frontinus. *Stratagems and Aqueducts*. Heinemann (Loeb Texts).

Miranda Green. *Roman Technology and Crafts*. Longman (Aspects of Roman Life series).
Pages 5–9, 24–26: arch construction and aqueducts. Written with the needs of school pupils in mind.

L.A. & J.A. Hamey. *The Roman Engineers*. Penguin Books.
Excellent sections on aqueducts: Ch. 2, pp. 8–18, also pp. 37–39.

Henry Hodges. *Technology of the Ancient World*. Allen Lane.
Pages 188–205: Roman engineering. A rather short account to do justice to the Roman achievement.

J.G. Landels. *Engineering in the Ancient World*. Chatto & Windus.

A.G. McKay. *Vitruvius: Architect and Engineer*. Macmillan.

H.V. Morton. *The Waters of Rome*. The Connoisseur and Michael Joseph. Although concerned with the fountains of Rome in general, has a chapter on the ancient aqueduct system.

E.M. Winslow. *A Libation to the Gods*. Hodder.
A readable yet detailed book on the aqueducts of Rome.

Audio-visual material

Appreciation of Architecture, 3: Roman Architecture. Visual Publications (Filmstrip).
Frames 1–16: arch construction (including aqueducts).
History of Western Art, Section 5: *Roman Art*. Visual Publications (Filmstrip).
Part 2, frames 1–18 are concerned with the arch leading on to gates, bridges and aqueducts.

7 Roman Food and Eating Habits

For detailed information on this topic, B. Flower and E. Rosenbaum's translation of Apicius' *A Roman Cookery Book* (Harrap) is perhaps the best reference book and contains many recipes.

Booklist

I. 8, p. 44	A brief paragraph.
I. 12, pp. 105–117	A good account angled towards Roman Britain, giving kind of food eaten and including some possible menus.
I. 13, p. 50	Meal – shown on tombstone.
I. 13, pp. 52–55	Eating and kitchen utensils.
I. 18, pp. 28–29	Simple and interesting account with menu.
I. 19, p. 37	Imaginative picture of evening meal.
I. 28, pp. 23–27	An imaginative reconstruction of a dinner party with most of the technical terms, menu and layout of **triclinium**.
I. 34, p. 46	Picture of a Roman reclining to eat, accompanying a very brief description of a simple meal.
I. 34, p. 39	Samian ware and glassware.
I. 34, p. 68	Kitchen implements.
I. 36, pp. 50–51	Two or three paragraphs.
I. 38, pp. 32–33	Two pages with illustrations.
I. 40, pp. 36–38	Pictures of a banquet, a kitchen and utensils.

I. 43, pp. 119–120	A concentrated paragraph giving the technical terms.
I. 46, pp. 59–67 & fig. 33	One or two good points can be got from this account but it requires careful selection before a pupil uses it.
I. 49, p. 32	Picture of a **triclinium** at Pompeii.
I. 49, p. 41	Mainly concerned with the food Romans did not have.
I. 50, p. 160	Relief showing Roman meal as in *The Roman Occupation of Britain* by I. Doncaster.
I. 57, pp. 164–167	A Romano-British kitchen and tableware.
I. 60, pp. 46–49	A very brief account.
I. 63, pp. 15–18	Very little information but a useful mention of mosaic on floor of **triclinium**.
I. 65, pp. 37–40	Brief text with illustrations – covers various aspects.
II. 2, pp. 108–112	A simply-written account containing most of the standard information and a little detail about food and tableware.
II. 3, pp. 287–300	The usual full and detailed account with many references and technical terms.
II. 4, pp. 90–95	An interesting account of the food of the ancient world with special reference to crops. Probably the best simple account.
II. 5, pp. 76–89	A fairly detailed account of Roman cooking relying heavily on Apicius.
II. 5, pp. 119–122	Milling and baking as an industry.
II. 5, pp. 122–123	Market gardening.
II. 10, pp. 201–205	A straightforward account of Roman eating habits.
II. 13, pp. 91–96	A short but thorough account.
II. 15, p. 65	The kitchen.
II. 15, Ch. 5	A good chapter on food generally.
II. 15, Ch. 6	Banquets including a description of furniture used.

II. 20, pp. 30–35	Various interesting quotations taken from original sources.
II. 27, pp. 209–212	A good deal of detail with many technical terms.
II. 29, pp. 173–175	Pliny's two letters about dinner parties.
III. 3, pp. 32–53	**Cena**.
III. 6, pp. 271–272	The woman's place at meals.
III. 13, plates 8–10	Pottery and utensils.
III. 13, plates 11–12	Baking and bakery industry.
III. 13, p. 105	Estimate of cost of feeding a slave.
III. 13, p. 282	A brief account of dinner parties.
III. 13, p. 326	The food of the common people.
III. 35, pp. 273–274	Remarks on **prandium**.
III. 35, pp. 277–284	**Cena** – a simple and readable account of the **cena** of Cicero's day.
III. 35, pp. 32 seq.	The food of the poorer classes.
III. 35, p. 48	The making of bread.
III. 35, p. 39	Water and wine.
IV. 2, pp. 69–80	Lavishly illustrated, with some useful points in the text.
IV. 4, p. 231	Two recipes.
IV. 4, pp. 233 seq.	Is about farming but suggests some of the things the Romans ate.
IV. 4, pp. 339–341	Luxurious dinners and cooking.
Illus. 44	A **commissatio**.
Illus. 217–225	Roman tableware.
IV. 6, pp. 85–86	Not a very detailed account but contains a worked-out menu.
IV. 7, pp. 154–161	An excellent account with a large amount of detail about Samian ware and tableware in general.

Additional books

Kenneth McLeish. *Food and Drink*. Allen & Unwin.
Marian Woodman. *Food and Cooking in Roman Britain*. Corinium Museum.
Simple and inexpensive booklet on this topic.

8 Education

Booklist

I. 1, pp. 10–11	Illustrations with brief text interspersed.
I. 8, pp. 47–48	A very brief summary.
I. 13, p. 40	Schoolmaster with pupils.
I. 18, pp. 18–19	Simple account with illustrations.
I. 24, pp. 26–35	Fairly detailed and useful account.
I. 28, pp. 7–11	First part deals with the **ludus litterarius**, the second with the school of the **grammaticus**. Contains a good deal of information about the kind of work done in schools.
I. 29, pp. 37–40	Deals with the ancient educational practices of the Romans, but not the schools.
I. 30, pp. 26–28	Four pages relate to education for children.
I. 35, pp. 50–54	A brief general account.
I. 38, pp. 34–35	Two pages with illustrations.
I. 39, p. 22	Brief reference with illustration
I. 43, pp. 112–113	Contains the basic information and technical terms.
I. 45, Ch. 3	A good account in simple terms and illustrated.
I. 49, pp. 54–55	A simple account. Pupils from modern primary schools might find 'yet the teaching was not really so different from today' rather misleading.
I. 57, pp. 58–65	A comprehensive account.
II. 2, pp. 114–116	Roman education as it might have applied to Britain.
II. 3, pp. 116–137	A very detailed account with a wealth of information within the framework of an attack on the system.
II. 4, pp. 277–279	A general account of the relationship between state and education.
II. 4, pp. 281–283	The influence of the family.

II. 4, pp. 285–287	The school of the **grammaticus**.
II. 4, pp. 289–291	Training for professions.
II. 5, pp. 35–45	A good simple account.
II. 6, Ch. 7	Rather more advanced account with wide ranging treatment of related subjects.
II. 10, pp. 153–160	A very blighting account of Roman education.
II. 13, pp. 64–73	A good and detailed account.
II. 15, pp. 167–173	A good account.
II. 17, pp. 72–80	Fairly full account in simple language.
II. 27, pp. 193–196	Good information with some Latin quotations.
II. 29, pp. 168–171	Pliny's letter about the school at Comum and a passage from Tacitus: *Dialogus*.
III. 2, pp. 215–220	An account of education in early Rome by Hugh Last with the emphasis on the role of the father and mother, the influence of religion and the aims in formation of character. Too difficult for pupils at this stage.
III. 3, pp. 92–106	A detailed account.
III. 7, pp. 211–215	This article by M.L. Clarke is concerned in the main with rhetoric but has a great deal of interesting material; pp. 219–225 are particularly concerned with the Roman schools. Quintilian's passage on the schoolmaster is quoted in translation.
III. 10, pp. 60–71	The importance of education under the Empire.
III. 13, pp. 310–311	A very brief account.
III. 14, p. 149	On Quintilian and Pliny.
III. 24, Vol. I, pp. 491–498	Passages from Suetonius, Valerius Maximus, Tacitus, Plutarch and Cicero.
III. 24, Vol. II, pp. 287–294	Passage from Quintilian, captions from the Elder Seneca.

III. 30, pp. 208–209	A short but concentrated summary.
III. 34, p. 26	The ideas of Cato.
III. 34, pp. 52–53	The coming of the Greek influence.
III. 35, pp. 168–203	Although long-winded, has some good material not easily found elsewhere.
IV. 2, pp. 59–68	A short account of education and much more about books and writing.
IV. 7, pp. 305–319	A clear and readable account containing the evidence for education in the Roman Empire, particularly in Gaul and Britain.

Additional books

W. Barclay. *Educational Ideals in the Ancient World.* Collins.
Ch. 4, 'Education among the Romans' is a very full and excellent account.

R. Barrow. *Greek and Roman Education.* Macmillan.
Excellent account suitable for middle school.

Stanley F. Bonner. *Education in Ancient Rome, from the Elder Cato to the Younger Pliny.* Methuen.
A definitive account.

E.B. Castle. *Ancient Education and Today.* Penguin. Ch. 4 is very full and good.

J.F. Dobson. *Ancient Education and its Meaning to Us: Our Debt to Greece and Rome.*
Ch. IV has a good and complete account from earliest stages.

A. Gwynn. *Roman Education from Cicero to Quintilian.* Oxford University Press. A very good book for reference, but rather too advanced for this stage.

J.A. Harrison. *Roman Education.* Bell & Hyman.
Neatly summarised account of education seen at its various stages through the eyes of a Roman boy.

Henry I. Marrou. *History of Education in Antiquity.* Sheed & Ward.
An important book on this topic.

Somerset Plantagenet Fry (ed.). *History in Pictures: The Roman World.* Macmillan.
Topics feature in this attractively-presented pictorial history and one of these covers a school scene. Naturally the book is to be regarded chiefly as a history.

Audio-visual material

People in Roman Times. EAV (Filmstrip).
Contains a few frames relating to this topic.

9 Roman Drama

Very little information is available in simple form. Most of the books in Booklist I have little more than a passing reference. Much information is available but often in a form which is rather difficult for pupils at this stage to read.

Booklist

I. 13, p. 35	Pictures of theatres at Verulamium and Orange.
I. 28, pp. 67–69	A short account with a description of a theatre.
I. 39, pp. 30–31, 35	Illustrations used to provide information and seek answers to questions. Interesting approach.
I. 43, pp. 139–141	A brief glance at writers and works.
pp. 142–145	Pictures relate to tragedy and comedy.
I. 45, pp. 70–71	Very brief comment and illustration.
I. 53, p. 7	Actors and the stage – mainly illustrations.
I. 60, p. 70	A short paragraph.
II. 2, pp. 71–72	A very brief account of the theatre in Britain.
II. 3, pp. 243–254	A detailed account in Carcopino's biting style – information for the teacher.
II. 5, p. 170	A brief paragraph.
II. 6, pp. 145–148	Main account with illustration facing p. 53.
II. 13, pp. 162–167	A reasonably full account.
II. 15, pp. 256–263	A worthwhile chapter with much technical detail.
II. 26, p. 116	Descriptions of Roman theatres. Illustrations are found on the following pages:

p. 35	Leptis Magna
p. 51	Timgad
p. 117	Aspendos
p. 118	Sabratha
p. 121	Orange
II. 27, pp. 167–169	A brief but detailed account with technical terms.
III. 1, pp. 68–95	Chapter devoted to Plautus and his works and less so to Terence – several passages quoted.
III. 3, pp. 270–288	A very useful account.
III. 20, pp. 19–34	The introduction to this book contains much information with emphasis on the differences between the Roman and the modern theatre.
III. 35, pp. 304–318	Much of interest.
IV. 2, pp. 151–162	A good, simple chapter with the usual excellent illustrations.
IV. 6, pp. 136–137	Useful for the illustrations.
IV. 7, pp. 367–376	Mainly a discussion of the theatre at Verulamium.

Additional books

S. Allott. *Plaudite*! Bell.

P. Arnott. *Introduction to the Greek Theatre*. Papermac.
Contains a chapter on Plautus with special reference to the Menaechmi.

W. Beare. *The Roman Stage*. Methuen.
Pages 164–195 might be useful for the teacher.

O.G. Brocket. *The Theatre*. Holt, Rinehart & Winston.
Part 2, Ch. 5 of this American book deals with the Roman theatre.

F.E. Brown. *Roman Architecture*. Studio Vista.
Illustrations 41–43 show Roman theatres.

J.J. Deiss. *The Town of Hercules: A Buried Treasure Trove*. Evans.
Ch. XIV deals with the theatre.

J. Wight Duff. *A Literary History of Rome*. Benn.
Deals with the whole field from a literary point of view.

H. & R. Leacroft. *The Buildings of Rome*. Brockhampton Press. Pages 26–29 are useful for pupils.
Kenneth McLeish. *Roman Comedy*. Macmillan.
Designed with certificate pupils in mind.
J. Allardyce Nicoll. *Development of the Theatre*. Harrap.
Early chapters deal with the Greek theatre and the Roman stage. Good photographs and plans.
D.S. Robertson. *Greek and Roman Architecture*. Cambridge University Press.
See especially pages 272–283 inclusive.
H.J. Rose. *Outlines of Classical Literature for Students of English*. Methuen.
F.H. Sandbach. *The Comic Theatre of Greece and Rome*. Chatto & Windus. A useful reference for teachers.
D. Taylor. *Acting and the Stage*. Allen & Unwin.
Designed with certificate pupils in mind.

Use might also be made of the Penguin translations of Plautus and Terence so that a scene might be acted.

Audio-visual material

The History of the European Theatre, 2: Roman. Visual Publications (Filmstrip). 44 frames, colour.
History of Western Art, Section 5: *Roman Art*. Visual Publications (Filmstrip).
Part 2, frames 22–28 well illustrate theatres at Jerash, Aspendos and Orange.

10 The Baths

Almost all the books give the same basic information and only a very few contain much more. The average account consists of a mention of **frigidarium, tepidarium** and **caldarium** and includes perhaps a picture of one of the rooms and a drawing of strigils. There is a dearth of good illustrations and J.J. Deiss *Herculaneum* (Souvenir Press) is the only book to try to take a set of baths and illustrate it, perhaps not entirely successfully.

Booklist

I. 10, pp. 43–44	A very brief account without details.
I. 12, pp. 44–45	Brief account with illustration of strigil and oil flask.
p. 46	Hypocausts with reconstruction.
I. 13, p. 28	Emphasis on noise, etc.
p. 31	Photographs of baths at Silchester with more detail.
p. 36	Photograph of Great Bath at Aquae Sulis with note.
I. 15, p. 73	Very brief references.
p. 98	Drawing of Roman baths at Bath.
I. 17, pp. 30–31	Brief but interesting section with a good cut-away illustration.
I. 18, pp. 24–25	Brief text with several illustrations and cut-away diagram.
I. 19, p. 26	Brief account.
p. 34	Illustration of bathers in the **frigidarium**.
I. 26, pp. 41–51	Interesting section on water and its use in the baths with illustrations and source material.
I. 28, pp. 21–23	Fairly detailed imaginative reconstruction.
I. 32, p. 133	Brief reference to Bath.
I. 33, pp. 61–64	Fairly detailed account with plan of baths at Wroxeter and sketch of hypocaust remains at Lincoln.
I. 34, pp. 36–37	Fairly detailed. Sketch of hypocaust, strigil and oil flask.
I. 35, pp. 38–39	Fairly detailed account of buildings and noise.
I. 37, pp. 28–31	Details of buildings.
I. 43, p. 119	Brief reference.
I. 45, p. 64	Very brief reference with illustration.
I. 46, pp. 34–36	Details of buildings and noise. Illustrations of strigil, Silchester and Bath.
I. 48, pp. 32–34	Plan of baths at Silchester and brief account.
I. 49, pp. 47–48	Brief account. Sketch of court of baths at Nîmes.
I. 50, p. 187	Photograph of remains of hypocaust at Bath.

I. 56,	p. 63	Plan of baths at Cadder.
	p. 65	Strigil.
	p. 66	Remains of hypocaust.
	p. 67	Reconstruction of hot room. Cold bath at Mumrills.
	pp. 63–69	Imaginative reconstruction of visit to baths with much detail.
I. 57,	p. 58	Brief description.
	pp. 126–127	Description of process of bathing. Sketch of hypocaust.
I. 60,	p. 42	Plan of **villa rustica** showing baths.
	pp. 45–46	Account includes description of Stabian baths at Pompeii.
I. 62,	pp. 59–60	Account includes reference to the baths of Caracalla and Diocletian with numbers.
I. 63,	p. 7	Plan of villa showing baths.
	p. 9	Diagram of a hypocaust.
	p. 14	Details of process of bathing.
II. 2,	p. 44	Military baths at Chesters on Hadrian's Wall.
	pp. 70–71	A simple account.
II. 3,	pp. 277–286	A most detailed account.
II. 5,	pp. 144–147	A short account.
II. 6,	pp. 93, 99–100 159–160, 171	Various references to the topic, especially pp. 159–160.
II. 10,	pp. 198–201	Mainly quotations from Carcopino.
II. 13,	pp. 169–170	A brief general account – no detail – quotes the well-known Seneca letter.
II. 15,	pp. 221–227	The usual detailed account.
II. 17,	pp. 101–104	Brief account of the **thermae** in action.
II. 27,	pp. 208–209	A short account, but has technical terms.
III. 3,	pp. 26–32	
III. 4,	pp. 131, 136, pp. 258–259	Various aspects of baths considered, both social and architectural.
III. 5,	pp. 26–32	A detailed account.
III. 6,	pp. 265–270	A very good detailed account.
III. 7,	pp. 275–276	A very brief account.
III. 35,	pp. 275–6	A limited account.

IV. 1 — A fair number of illustrations and mention in the text of specific buildings.
IV. 2, pp. 91–102 — Interesting text and good illustrations.
IV. 4, p. 337 — Little in text on this subject.
pp. 291–292 — Concerned with the baths as buildings.
pp. 137–140 — Illustrations.

Additional book

J.J. Deiss. *The Town of Hercules: A Buried Treasure Trove*. Evans.
Pages 111–119 describe the baths.

Audio-visual material

Appreciation of Architecture: 3, Roman. Visual Publications (Filmstrip).
Frames 17–22 and 24–25 provide useful photographs and cut-away diagrams.

History of Western Art, Section 5: *Roman Art*. Visual Publications (Filmstrip).
Part 3, frames 1–20 examine in detail with several reconstructions of the great **thermae** in Rome.

Aquae Sulis. Ginn (Slides).
Several slides relate to the Roman baths at Bath.

11 Amphitheatres and the Circus

Booklist

I. 1, pp. 16–17 — Simple and lively text accompanies numerous illustrations of Circus and amphitheatre.
I. 10, p. 45 — A very brief mention.
I. 12, pp. 80–84 — On the entertainment of Roman crowds generally.
I. 13, pp. 32–33 — Illustrations of amphitheatres and gladiators.
I. 15, pp. 34–36 — Brief account, but includes drawing of gladiator's equipment.

I. 19, p. 14	A drawing of an amphitheatre.
I. 22, p. 24	Brief but informative accounts of the Colosseum and the Circus, each with illustration.
I. 26, pp. 35–40	Short section on amphitheatre with illustrations and original source material.
I. 28, pp. 63–73	Good detail in a fictional discussion between Publius and the door-keeper who had been a gladiator.
I. 33, pp. 67–69	A brief mention of Roman entertainment as it applies in Britain.
I. 34, pp. 12–15	The amphitheatre at Caerleon and what might have happened there.
I. 35, pp. 40–43	A simple account.
I. 37, pp. 57–65	A simple yet fairly detailed account.
I. 39, pp. 26–29, 33, 35	Brief but informative account with illustrations for Circus and amphitheatre.
I. 40, pp. 18–19	Has good photographs.
I. 43, pp. 120–121	Very brief mention of public entertainment and a more detailed description of Roman dice.
I. 45, pp. 65–69	Brief account covering various aspects with several illustrations.
I. 46, pp. 101–102	Some good information.
I. 48, p. 26	Plan of Caerleon amphitheatre.
I. 49, pp. 43–47	A very brief account.
I. 52, p. 115	Line drawing of gladiators from a relief of Pompeii.
I. 53, pp. 8–9	Gladiators, horse-racing and hunting – mainly illustrations.
I. 54, pp. 36–38	Some useful line drawings. Also an account of Spartacus.
I. 60, pp. 65–72	Gladiators are dealt with on pp. 70–72.
I. 61, pp. 47–49	Brief account with illustration of Circus and amphitheatre.
I. 62, pp. 68–69	The Colosseum.
II. 2, pp. 72–74	A brief account.

II. 3,	pp. 254 seq.	Deals in great detail with public amusements: pp. 254 seq. with the amphitheatre. Private amusements are dealt with on pp. 271–276.
II. 4,	pp. 157–158	A brief account.
II. 5,	pp. 173–179	Includes a fair amount of detail in the shape of an account of a day at the amphitheatre.
II. 6,	pp. 145–146, 149–152, 157, 171	Useful and informative references to both Circus and amphitheatre.
II. 13,	pp. 153–162	A good detailed account.
II. 15,	pp. 249–254	A good account.
	pp. 232–240	Deals with private pastimes.
II. 17,	pp. 105–114	Fairly detailed and interesting account of the Circus and the amphitheatre – few illustrations.
II. 26,	pp. 119–124	Some useful illustrations of amphitheatres.
II. 27,	pp. 161–173	A bare account with technical terms.
III. 3,	pp. 244–270	Games and entertainment.
III. 5,	pp. 255–261,	Detail on buildings and entertainment generally.
	pp. 333–335	
III. 7,	pp. 279–281	
III. 14,	pp. 233–244	A detailed account with much interesting information.
III. 24,	Vol. II pp. 229–230	Some relevant quotations.
III. 35,	pp. 302–304	A brief account of the situation in Cicero's time.
IV. 1,	p. 66	The amphitheatre.
	p. 200	A gladiator's helmet.
IV. 2,	pp. 163–174	Information about amphitheatres and gladiators, well illustrated.
IV. 4,	pp. 283–286	Description of amphitheatres. Illustrations on pp. 148–161 are excellent.
	pp. 329–335	Gladiators.
IV. 6,	pp. 45–55	Some excellent illustrations.
IV. 7,	pp. 370–380	Usual detail applying both to Roman Britain and far beyond.
IV. 12,	p. 167	Some illustrations of gladiatorial shows.

Additional books

Arena: The Story of the Colosseum. Thames and Hudson.
A fascinating book for reference.

Roland Auguet. *Cruelty and Civilization: The Roman Games.* Panther.

David Buchanan. *Roman Sport and Entertainment.* Longman.
One of the Aspects series with illustrations and questions.

M. Grant. *Gladiators.* Weidenfeld & Nicolson.
Probably the most detailed and best account.

H. & R. Leacroft. *Buildings of Ancient Rome.* Brockhampton Press. Useful illustrations.

David P. Mannix. *Those About to Die: The Full Story of the Roman Games.* Mayflower.

Peter Quennell. *The Colosseum.* Reader's Digest.

D.S. Robertson. *Greek and Roman Architecture.* Cambridge University Press.
See especially pages 283–289 inclusive.

Mortimer Wheeler and V.E. Nash Williams. *Caerleon Roman Amphitheatre and Prysg Field Barrack Buildings, Monmouthshire.* HMSO.

For extra information on buildings

F.E. Brown. *Roman Architecture.* Studio Vista.
Photographs on pages 46–49 are useful.

D.R. Dudley. *Urbs Roma.* Phaidon.
Pages 142–145 have quotations referring to the amphitheatre.
Pages 211–216 have quotations referring to the Circus Maximus.

Audio-visual material

Appreciation of Architecture, 3: Roman. Visual Publications.
Several frames relate to Colosseum, baths, theatres and temples.

Greek and Roman Sports. Educational Audio-Visual Ltd.
Filmstrip 2, with cassette, is relevant here.

History of Western Art, Section 5: *Roman Art.* Visual Publications.
Part 2: frames 20, 21 illustrate the amphitheatre at Jerash, while 29–34 examine closely the Colosseum and its construction.

12 Coming of Age

Booklist

I. 37, p. 19	
II. 10, p. 159	Very brief account.
II. 13, p. 74	
II. 20, pp. 17–18	A variety of quotations on the subject from original sources.
III. 3, pp. 120–121	
III. 5, pp. 119–120	

13 Weddings

Booklist

I. 24, pp. 17–25	A useful and interesting section with illustrations, source material and suggested activities.
I. 43, pp. 108–112	Marriage described in some detail.
p. 112	Birth and childhood.
I. 45, p. 11	A cursory comment on the subject with sketch.
I. 46, pp. 83–84	Short account.
I. 57, pp. 165–169	Home life in Roman Britain. 'Marriage' rather than 'wedding', but interesting.
I. 60, Ch. 8	Marriage and funeral customs. Illustration of a funeral and a **columbarium**.
I. 65, p. 34	Brief reference with illustration.
II. 3, Ch. 4	Detailed account of marriage, women and the family.
p. 87	Description of a wedding ceremony.
II. 4, pp. 144–147	Position of women.
II. 5, Ch. 3	Includes death and burial as well as marriage and life in the home.
II. 6, pp. 82–83	Brief but informative account.
II. 10, pp. 144–151	Includes an account of women's place in the home. Two epitaphs quoted.
II. 13, pp. 59–66	
II. 17, pp. 61–63	Brief but comprehensive account.

II. 20, pp. 6–9	Various aspects treated by reference to original source material.
III. 2, pp. 220–227	Position of women.
III. 6, pp. 173–189	A good chapter on the subject.
pp. 200–223	Deals with happy and unhappy marriages and with divorce.
III. 24, Vol. I, pp. 59–60	Some relevant quotations.
III. 35, Ch. 5	Deals with marriage and the position of the **materfamilias**.

Additional book

J.A. Crook. *Law and Life of Rome*. Thames and Hudson. Ch. 6 contains a detailed account of legal aspects of marriage.

14 Funerals

Booklist

I. 24, pp. 55–62	A useful and fairly detailed section with illustrations, source material and suggested activities.
I. 39, p. 8	Interesting illustration employed for putting questions and supplying information.
I. 43, p. 122	A brief account.
I. 45, pp. 89–91	Very brief comment and illustrations.
I. 46, pp. 84–87	Illustration of funeral and brief account.
I. 60, pp. 75–80	
II. 5, pp. 91–94	
II. 6, p. 84	Very brief account of the subject.
II. 13, pp. 80–85	
II. 15, Ch. 11	
II. 20, p. 36	Interesting selection of quotations on the subject from original sources.
III. 3, pp. 126–129	

Additional book

J.M.C. Toynbee. *Death and Burial in the Roman World*. Thames & Hudson.

15 Clientes

Booklist

I. 24, p. 15	Roman society described – **clientes** referred to but not named.
II. 6, pp. 47–48, 96	Brief references to the position of **cliens** and **patronus**.
II. 10, pp. 196–197	
II. 13, p. 80	
II. 24, p. 15	Origin and development.
III. 4, pp. 23, 45, 247, 257	Various aspects of **clientela** are referred to.
III. 11, p. 11	A brief explanation of the relationship between **cliens** and **patronus**.
III. 16, pp. 42–43	Relationship of **cliens** and **patronus** is briefly described.
III. 28, p. v	A brief account is supplied here.

Audio-visual material

Roman Society. Educational Audio-Visual Ltd (Filmstrip).
A single frame (25) and the accompanying commentary refer to **clientela**.

16 Pompeii

Booklist

I. 25, pp. 1–8	Chapter devoted to Pompeii with maps and diagrams, photographs and use of source material. Suggested activities supplied.
IV. 1	This book is well illustrated and deals in some detail with both Pompeii and Herculaneum.

Additional books

Ian Andrews. *Pompeii*. Cambridge University Press.
Fully illustrated and intended for school use.

P. Connolly. *Pompeii*. Macdonald.
Fully illustrated and designed with pupils in mind.

Alfonso de Franciscis. *The Buried Cities: Pompeii and Herculaneum*. Orbis.
Fairly brief text with splendid and numerous illustrations.
Michael Grant. *Cities of Vesuvius: Pompeii and Herculaneum*. Hamlyn.
P. Grimal. *In Search of Ancient Italy*. Evans Bros. Ch. 6.
P. MacKendrick. *The Mute Stones Speak*. Methuen.
A. Maiuri. *Pompeii*. Bailey Bros.
Well illustrated. Detailed description.
Raleigh Trevelyan. *The Shadow of Vesuvius: Pompeii A.D. 79*. Michael Joseph.
An unusual and interesting presentation with numerous illustrations.
R.J. Unstead. *Living in Pompeii*. A. & C. Black.
Illustrated with artist's drawings; intended for school use.

Audio-visual material

Appreciation of Architecture, 3: Roman. Visual Publications (Filmstrip).
Covers Pompeii, baths, temples and theatres.
Herculaneum. Kay (Filmstrip).
A fairly recent and interesting publication with many frames of relevance for Pompeii.
History of Western Art, Section 5: Roman Art. Visual Publications (Filmstrip).
Part 5 (36 colour frames). High quality illustrations with good notes consider Pompeii in various aspects: streets and buildings, theatre and arena, houses, decoration and domestic objects.
Pompeii. BBC Radiovision (Filmstrip).
Pompeii. Gateway (Filmstrip).
29 colour frames. High quality photographs illustrate the topic most successfully.
Pompeii and Herculaneum. Visual Information Services (Filmstrip).
34 colour frames, grouped to illustrate buildings, streets, houses and decoration.
Buried Pompeii. Pictorial Colour Slides.
A very useful collection of 30 slides with some less usual items. A set of 15 slides, *Buried Herculaneum*, is available in the same series.

Pompeii and Herculaneum. Woodmansterne (Slides).
18 high-quality colour slides illustrate various aspects of life in the towns.
Roman Art: Painting. Audio Visual Productions (Slides)
48 colour slides. A valuable collection of mosaics and wall paintings – particularly well represented are the House of the Vettii and the Villa of the Mysteries.
A Roman House. Audio Visual Publications (Slides).
24 colour slides. Almost all the places, objects and pictures relate to Pompeii and Herculaneum.
Pompeii. Daily Telegraph (Wallchart).
Pompeii. Pictorial Education No. 7 (Wallchart).
Historical Reconstructions of Pompeii. Encyclopaedia Britannica.
Set of 4 prints with overlays illustrate house, bakery, theatre and temple.

17 Religion

Booklist

I.17, pp. 32–33, 43	A useful section covering the old gods, temples and sacrifice and Christianity.
I. 22, pp. 36–42	Short but informative accounts of the various types of gods, with special attention to Mithras and the Christians. A section relates to prophecy – all with illustrations.
I. 26, pp. 30–34	Section devoted to temple types in Roman Britain followed by suggested class activities.
I. 31, pp. 26, 38, 44–45	The old religion, its weaknesses and the rise of Christianity.
I. 43, pp. 125–131	A detailed and fairly demanding account.
I. 45, pp. 77–89	Brief accounts of various aspects with illustrations.
I. 53, pp. 24–25	Many aspects illustrated with very brief note.

I. 61, pp. 45–46	Brief account with illustrations.
II. 17, pp. 19–27	Informative treatment of the subject – few illustrations.
III. 1, pp. 97 seq.	Many aspects of Roman religion and later philosophy are considered.
III. 3, pp. 121–126	
III. 9, pp. 48, 108–109, 198, 311, 397–401, 483–488, 545–549	Numerous references to the position of religion at various periods of Roman history.
III. 18, pp. 213–261	A comprehensive account of religion in the Empire.
III. 21, pp. 154–188	A detailed survey of the subject.

Additional books

David Birt. *Religion in Roman Britain*. Longman.
Part of the history unit *The Romans in Britain*, a useful source with activities.

J. Ferguson. *The Religions of the Roman Empire*. Thames & Hudson.

Michael Massey. *Roman Religion*. Longman.
One of the Aspects series with illustrations and class activities.

R.M. Ogilvie. *The Romans and Their Gods in the Age of Augustus*. Chatto & Windus.
A useful book for teacher reference.

D.S. Robertson. *Greek and Roman Architecture*. Cambridge University Press.
Chapters 13 and 14 deal with temple architecture in Republic and Empire.

John Sharwood Smith. *Temples, Priests and Worship*. Allen & Unwin.
Relates to Greece and Rome and designed with schools in mind.

Audio-visual material

Appreciation of Architecture, Part 3; Roman Architecture. Visual Publications (Filmstrip).
Frames 26–35 provide black and white illustrations of various types of temple with sections.
History of Western Art, Section 5: Roman Art (Filmstrips).
Part 1 (41 colour frames): from frame 15 onwards, various temples and religious sites are illustrated, including Palmyra, Petra, Baalbek and Tivoli. Part 3, frames 22–28 examine the Pantheon in some detail.
Life in Roman Britain: Religion. Audio Visual Productions No. 5006.
3 OHP transparencies plus a text for teacher reference.
Religion in Roman Life. Educational Audio-Visual Ltd.
Filmstrip and cassette: a useful production on the subject.

18 Army

Booklist

I. 13, pp. 13–25	
I. 17, pp. 18–19	Brief but useful account with illustrations.
I. 31, pp. 12–13, 31–36	Early and imperial army discussed with useful illustrations.
I. 57, Ch. 6	
I. 60, pp. 4–20	
II. 2, Ch. 3	

Additional books

P. Connolly. *The Roman Army.* Macdonald Educational.
Splendidly illustrated and suitable for school use.
L. Cottrell. *The Great Invasion.* Evans. Ch. 4.
G.R. Dudley & G. Webster. *The Rebellion of Boudicca.* Routledge & Kegan Paul. Ch. 2.
FLARE Education Group. *Lincoln in Roman Times: The Roman Army.* Flare. A comprehensive and interesting production.
Michael Grant. *The Army of the Caesars.* Weidenfeld & Nicolson.
Detailed account for teacher reference.

Peter Hodge. *The Roman Army*. Longman.
One of the Aspects series with plentiful illustration and suggested activities.
Matthew Holden. *The Legions of Rome*. Wayland.
Well illustrated and designed with pupils in mind.
H. Russell Robinson. *Armour of Imperial Rome*. Arms and Armour Press.
Splendidly illustrated and an important point of reference.
Michael Simkins. *The Roman Army from Caesar to Trajan*. Osprey.
Michael Simkins. *The Roman Army from Hadrian to Constantine*. Osprey.
Well illustrated books with historical development particularly in mind.
G.R. Watson. *The Roman Soldier*. Thames & Hudson. (Aspects of Greek & Roman Life series).
G. Webster. *The Roman Army*. Grosvenor Museum, Chester.
G. Webster. *The Roman Imperial Army of the First and Second Centuries*. A. & C. Black.

Audio-visual material

Caesar's Army. Educational Audio-Visual Ltd (Filmstrip). Two filmstrips, colour.
The Roman Army. Common Ground (Filmstrip). 30 frames, black and white.
The Roman Army. Educational Audio-Visual Ltd. (Filmstrip). 35 frames, colour.
Roman Britain: Fortifications. Baddeley (Filmstrip). 25 frames, colour.
The Roman Occupation: Fortifications. Gateway (Filmstrip). 37 frames, colour.
The Roman Occupation: Weapons. Gateway (Filmstrip). 20 frames, colour.
The Roman Army. Sunday Times (Wallchart).

The Scottish Development Department have produced six colour slides on the Roman soldier (Nos. 238–243).